THE VICTORIA AND ALBERT COLOUR BOOKS

FIRST PUBLISHED IN GREAT BRITAIN BY
WEBB & BOWER (PUBLISHERS) LIMITED
9 COLLETON CRESCENT, EXETER, DEVON EX2 4 BY
AND MICHAEL JOSEPH LIMITED, 27 WRIGHTS LANE, LONDON W8 5TZ
IN ASSOCIATION WITH THE VICTORIA AND ALBERT MUSEUM, LONDON

FIRST PUBLISHED 1987
SECOND IMPRESSION MAY 1987
THIRD IMPRESSION AUGUST 1987
FOURTH IMPRESSION MARCH 1988

BOOK, COVER AND SLIP CASE DESIGN BY CARROLL, DEMPSEY & THIRKELL
LIMITED

BRITISH LIBRARY CATALOGUING IN PUBLICATION DATA

YOUNG, HILARY
PATTERNS FOR TEXTILES-(THE VICTORIA AND ALBERT COLOUR BOOKS)
1. TEXTILE DESIGN
1. TITLE II. SERIES
746 NK8805

ISBN 0-86350-150-8

PRODUCTION BY FACER PUBLISHING
COLOUR REPRODUCTION BY PENINSULAR REPRO SERVICE, EXETER
TYPESET IN GREAT BRITAIN BY OPTIC

PRINTED AND BOUND IN HONG KONG BY
MANDARIN OFFSET

THE VICTORIA AND ALBERT COLOUR BOOKS

# PATTERNS FOR TEXTILES

INTRODUCTION BY
HILARY YOUNG

WEBB & BOWER
MICHAEL JOSEPH
MCMLXXXVII

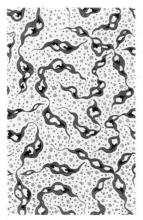 IN 1986 the Victoria and Albert Museum was particularly fortunate to be able to purchase three albums of designs and patterns for printed textiles which can be attributed to Mulhouse, a town on the French border with Germany, or to a nearby region on the Rhine, the present day French *département* of Upper Alsace. The albums contain nearly 800 designs and prints, and their compiler has often pasted similar patterns on to the same page; consequently, many pages bear designs that differ widely in date. The albums themselves are contained within portfolios labelled *Ornements des Tissus* and they were probably assembled in the latter part of the nineteenth century. Their contents, however, range in date from about 1775 to the middle of the nineteenth century, and in terms of quality they far surpass the Museum's earlier acquisitions of Continental textile designs of that age.

The earliest textile printworks at Mulhouse, that of Koechlin, Schmaltzer et Cie, was established in 1747. In setting up the firm the proprietors took advantage of the town's position on the BasleLorraine trade route and of its own natural resources – copious supplies of fresh water and fields for washing and drying goods in. The printworks at Basle had at this date an export market for their goods in Lorraine and Frankfurt which they failed to expand to meet – a situation propitious for the development of textile printing twenty miles away at Mulhouse. Following the establishment of printworks in this town production spread to Upper Alsace, and these developments have been thoroughly researched and documented by the successive curators of the Musée de l'Impression sur Etoffes de Mulhouse (see Bibliography). The Musée at Mulhouse houses a very rich collection of documented designs and printed textiles produced in this region, and it is by stylistic comparison with these that the attribution of the designs in this book to this area of eastern France has been made.

Among the designs are several that are almost identical to surviving designs from the firm of Risler and Koechlin of Mulhouse, and others are very close to cottons printed by Haussman Frères of Logelbach. Possibly, here as elsewhere, manufacturers may have copied one another's products and employed the same designers. That the latter is the case is suggested by the presence in the albums of designs (illustrated in *Floral Borders*, a companion book in the series) by Louis-Albert Du Bois, an artist who is known to have supplied designs to the Fabrique de Fazy aux Bergues, Geneva, and of others identical in style to designs associated with the major textile centre of Jouy in France *(plates 14-16)*. Clearly, the designs must have

formed part of an archive of patterns and designs of one or more printworks, though the identity of these printworks remains to be established.

The albums contain both original designs in watercolour and bodycolour, and impressions on paper taken from the woodblocks and engraved copperplates used to print the fabric. Many of the designs are numbered, but their numbering does not follow a precise chronological sequence. Some are annotated in French, others in German (or in both of these languages), and three are inscribed in Italian. These inscriptions lend a further measure of support to the attribution to Mulhouse and Alsace, since both are situated near the German and Swiss departs.

The earliest patterns in the albums are impressions taken from engraved copperplates and can be dated to the late 1770s. The technique of printing

C

cotton from engraved copperplates had been introduced in Ireland by Francis Nixon in 1752, and after the legalizing of textile printing in France in 1759 textile designers fully exploited the potential of the printing plate to reproduce highly detailed, large-scale, pictorial designs. During the last quarter of the century the fashion for pictorial patterns declined, and these impressions are less ambitious in design, being composed of intertwining floral trails or of stripes alternating with bouquets, cornucopiae, or vignettes (plates 1 and 2).

Closely related in style to these impressions is a group of thirty-six original designs preserved in the albums. These are executed in red watercolour and many of them are inscribed in German and one in French. Typical examples are reproduced in plate 3. At first sight it would appear that the design of meandering plant trails was for a plate-printed cotton. Some of the designs, however, have areas of solid colour – an effect that could not be reproduced from an engraved copperplate, but one obtainable from a wooden printing block. Furthermore, the sizes of the repeats are closer to those found on block-printed textiles, and it therefore seems likely that these designs were intended to be realized as block-printed textiles.

The first successful European attempts at block-printing in fast colours

on cotton had been made in emulation of imported Indian painted cottons. By the end of the seventeenth century European printers had discovered and adapted for textile printing the Indian technique of painting a mordant – that is a substance which enabled the fabric to take the dye – onto cotton and then subsequently dyeing the piece in madder, which resulted in a range of reds and browns. Throughout the eighteenth century, and during the one that followed, designers were much influ-enced by the patterns of Indian textiles. The designs of exotic plants in plates 9 to 11, for example, are adapted from the pat-terns of Indian painted cottons, but are here laid over the dark grounds fashionable during the last two decades of the eighteenth century.

By the date that these designs were drawn, European printed textiles had attained a level of sophistication such that they could compete successfully for the custom of fashionable clients with figured silks. As is apparent from many designs in the albums, in competing for a share of this market the designers were prepared to imitate the products of their rivals, the silk mercers; the small designs in plate 26 and text figure B all have small ragged-edged motifs derived from the patterns of warp-printed silks. Similarly, the striped patterns which had been introduced in printed cottons by the 1770s, and which continued to be popular until the last decade of the century, had their origins in the patterns of figured silks *(plates 5 to 8)*.

The printworks of Mulhouse and Alsace also looked to rival printworks elsewhere in western Europe. Among the designs in the albums are a number *(see plates 14-16)* that are very close in style to others preserved at Mulhouse. These are associated with the major textile centre of Jouy in

France. These date from the 1790s and are of small sprigs scattered on dark grounds. Like many drawings in the collection, some of these show alternative treatments for the ground pattern. This type of design, when reduced in scale so that the motifs were closer to each other, also served as filling patterns for printed shawls and handkerchiefs of the late eighteenth century. A number of these designs for filling patterns are reproduced here, together with later variations on the same theme *(plates 17 and 18)*; designs similar to those with green grounds in plate 18 were made for the firm of Risler and Koechlin of Mulhouse in 1807.

Until the first decade of the nineteenth century textile printing had largely been based on the use of vegetable dyes. During the first third of the century mineral colours were developed, and their intended effect can be seen in many of the designs reproduced between plates 21 and 30. With their arresting combinations of bright reds, greens, and yellows, the 'Cashmere' patterns reproduced in plate 21 must have been intended for printing with the new mineral colours, used here in combination with the technique of

discharge printing. By this technique pigment is removed from a fabric with a printed discharge, and, after subsequent dyeing, the 'discharged' areas take up the colour of the secondary dyeing. These designs date from about 1810 and, incidentally, testify to the continuing influence of Indian textiles. Text figure C, a pattern of serpentine trails of branching stems, dates from about 1805-10 and shows a type of design that was to enjoy considerable popularity until the 1820s. In two related designs of the mid-1820s the branching stems are laid over rollerprinted 'rainbow' stripes *(plate 16, top centre and plate 17, bottom centre)*.

The designs and impressions of the following two decades are in a wide variety of styles, but two major trends can be discerned: naturalism and floral stylization. Sometimes, as in the designs with brown grounds in plate 27 and 28, the two were combined within a single drawing. Many designers were eclectic in their approach; the angular lines of the plant stems in two of these drawings are derived from Indian shawls, and other designs show the influence of Islamic patterns *(plate 29, top left and bottom right)*. Among the designs dating from the second quarter of the nineteenth century are many of flower heads set on pale, lightly patterned grounds and these are of a type that is still popular today *(plates 29 and 30)*.

The albums contain a group of twenty-seven block impressions which are printed with bold patterns in red and black or brown *(plates 31 and 32)*. These are among the most difficult patterns to date, for many of their designs recall patterns produced in the eighteenth century – those in imitation of leopard skin for example *(text figure D)*. However, a number of these impressions include devices derived from Islamic calligraphy, and this suggests a date a little after the middle of the nineteenth century. If this is right, then the prints are among the latest patterns in the albums. The collection also includes a large number of designs for printed borders, among which number some of the most striking images in the collection, and these are discussed and illustrated separately in *Floral Borders*, a companion volume in this series.

BIBLIOGRAPHY

Albrecht-Mathey, E, *The Fabrics of Mulhouse and Alsace, 1750-1800*, Leigh-on-Sea, 1968.

Thomé Jacqué, J, *Chefs d'œuvre du Musée de l'Impression sur Etoffes, Mulhouse*, three volumes, Tokyo, 1978.

Tuchscherer, J M, *The Fabrics of Mulhouse and Alsace, 1801-1850*, Leigh-on-Sea, 1972.

Thomé Jacqué, J, *Chefs d'œuvre du Musée de l'Impression sur Etoffes, Mulhouse*, three volumes, Tokyo, 1978.

Much help was given in the preparation of this book by Miss Natalie Rothstein.

### KEY TO PLATES

All works illustrated are in watercolour and/or bodycolour unless otherwise stated.

*1.* top, late 1770s (impression from engraved copperplate); bottom, 1790s. *2.* late 1770s (impressions from engraved copperplates). *3.* 1780s-90s. *4.* top, 1790s; bottom 1780s-90s. *5.* top, c.1790; bottom c.1780. *6.* 1780s-90s. *7-11.* 1790s. *12.* top 1790s; bottom, c.1800 (impression from woodblock). *13-15.* c.1795-1800. *16.* c.1795-1800; top centre c.1825; 2nd row right 1820s. *17.* dark ground designs c.1800; green ground designs c.1805-10; bottom centre c.1825. *18.* c.1800-10; top left and right c.1795-1800. *19-20.* c.1810-15. *21.* c.1810. *22.* top c.1820-30; middle left and right, and bottom c.1820-30, middle centre c.1830-40. *23.* top left c.1800-10; top right c.1810-20; 2nd row left and right 1830s; 2nd row centre 1820s; top and bottom centre 1820s; the remainder c.1825-50. *24.* c.1820-50; 2nd row centre c.1795-1800; 2nd row left and right c.1825. *25.* top left c.1815-20; top right and bottom left c.1830-40; bottom right c.1800. *26.* top c.1800; middle c.1795-1800; bottom c.1820-30. *27.* top c.1820-30; bottom left c.1830-40; bottom right c.1840. *28.* top left c.1830; top right and bottom left c.1830-40; bottom right c.1840. *29.* top left and bottom right c.1850; top right c.1840; bottom left c.1820-30. *30.* bottom right c.1800 (impression from woodblocks); top left c.1845-50; top right c.1825-35; bottom left c.1840. *31.* Impressions from woodblocks: left c.1800; right c.1850-60. *32.* top left c.1795-1800; bottom c.1830-40; right c.1850-60 (impressions from woodblocks).

THE PLATES

1

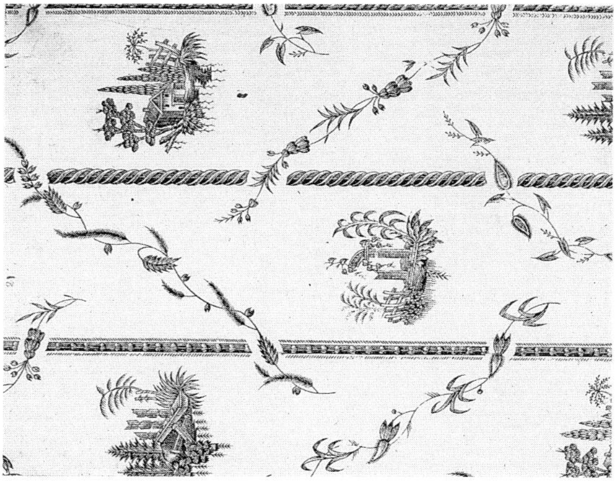

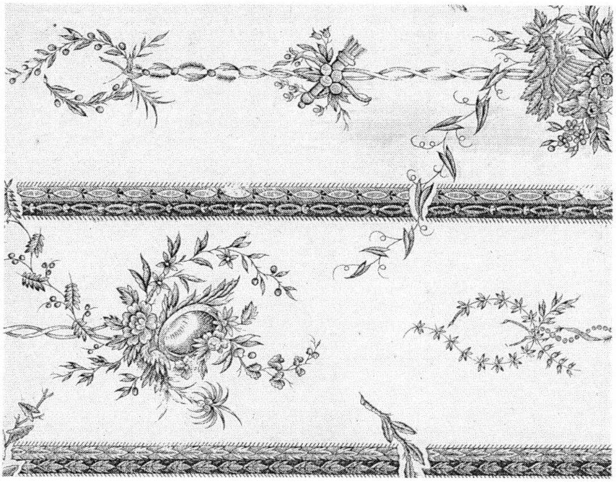

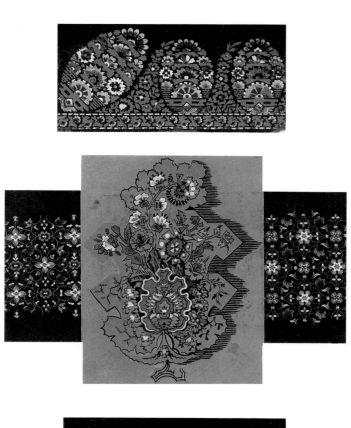

23

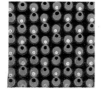

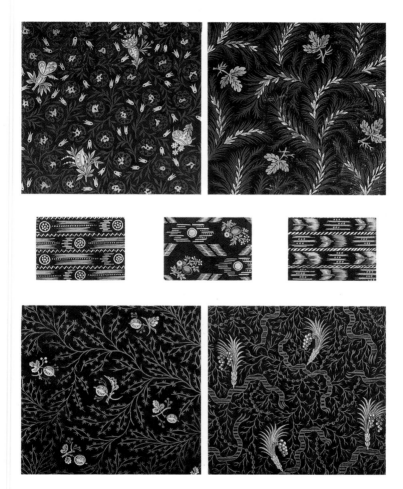

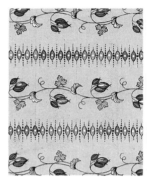

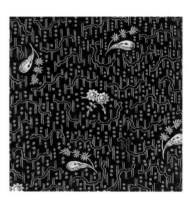

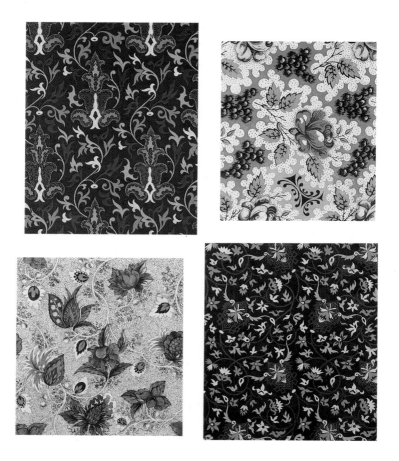

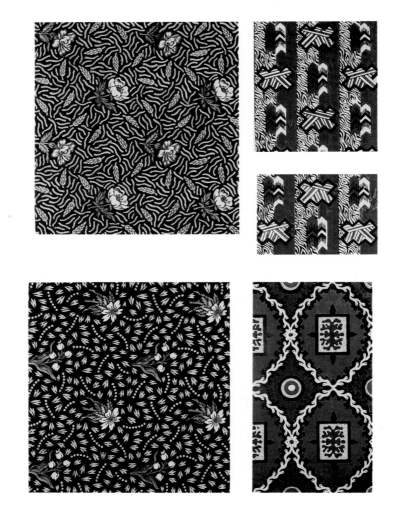